AF270471

IDITAROD TRAIL INVITATIONAL

LUKE HANLON

SportsZore

An Imprint of Abdc Publishing
abdobooks.com

abdobooks.com

Published by Abdo Publishing, a division of ABDO, PO Box 398166, Minneapolis, Minnesota 55439. Copyright © 2024 by Abdo Consulting Group, Inc. International copyrights reserved in all countries. No part of this book may be reproduced in any form without written permission from the publisher. SportsZone™ is a trademark and logo of Abdo Publishing.

Printed in the United States of America, North Mankato, Minnesota.
102023
012024

Cover Photo: Dan Bailey/Alaska Stock/Design Pics Inc/Alamy
Interior Photos: Dan Bailey/Alaska Stock/Design Pics Inc/Alamy, 4–5, 13, 17, 21, 24–25; Red Line Editorial, 7; Ron Levy/ZUMA Wire/Cal Sport Media/AP Images, 9; The Times/News Licensing/MEGA/NEWSUK/Newscom, 11; Sam Harrel/Fairbanks Daily News-Miner/ZUMA Press/Alamy Live News/Alamy, 14; Al Grillo/Alaska Stock/Design Pics Inc/Alamy, 16; NB/TRAN/Alamy, 18–19, 23, 27, 28

Editor: Steph Giedd
Series Designer: Cynthia Della-Rovere

Library of Congress Control Number: 2023939477

Publisher's Cataloging-in-Publication Data

Names: Hanlon, Luke, author.
Title: Iditarod Trail Invitational / by Luke Hanlon
Description: Minneapolis, Minnesota: ABDO Publishing, 2024 | Series: Extreme sports events | Includes online resources and index.
Identifiers: ISBN 9781098292362 (lib. bdg.) | ISBN 9798384910305 (ebook)
Subjects: LCSH: Extreme sports--Juvenile literature. | Action sports (Extreme sports)--Juvenile literature. | Ultra-marathon running--Juvenile literature. | Running races--Juvenile literature. | All terrain bicycling--Juvenile literature. | Skis and skiing--Juvenile literature. | Winter sports--Juvenile literature.
Classification: DDC 796.046--dc23

TABLE OF CONTENTS

CHAPTER 1

NEVER GIVE UP

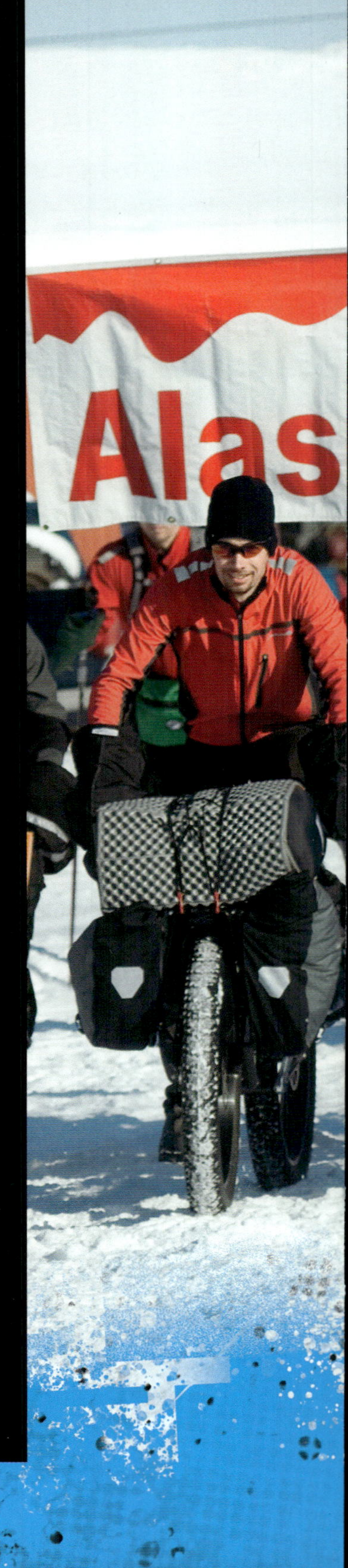

Pete Ripmaster had completed a race at the Iditarod Trail Invitational (ITI) before. Though he could have chosen to either bike or ski, Ripmaster completed the 350-mile (563-km) course on foot. That made him want to test himself further. In 2016 he set out on foot to conquer the longer ITI course, which stretches 1,000 miles (1,609 km).

About 200 miles (322 km) into the course, Ripmaster came across an ice bridge on a river. Using his hiking poles, Ripmaster poked the bridge to see if it was stable. Once he was halfway across, he heard cracking under his feet. The bridge collapsed and sent him into the freezing waters of the river.

Ripmaster barely escaped drowning. After trekking another 300 miles (483 km), he

Both the ITI 350 and 1,000 races begin in Anchorage, Alaska.

knew he wouldn't be able to finish the race, so he dropped out. He tried the 1,000-mile course again in 2017. The temperatures reached −65 degrees Fahrenheit (−54°C) and caused some competitors to lose fingers and toes from frostbite. Ripmaster became fearful that he could die from competing in such harsh conditions. Once again, he withdrew from the race.

Despite the consecutive failures, Ripmaster returned to the trail once again in 2018. He promised himself this would be his final attempt to finish the almost monthlong journey across Alaska. Nearly 800 miles (1,287 km) into his journey, Ripmaster was in tears and close to giving up again. But while he was walking through a town on the trail, he met a local who convinced him to keep going. Ripmaster talked to the man and even met his family. After that, his energy was renewed. He crossed the finish line in 26 days, 13 hours, and 44 minutes. "I was sick, I was tired, but all I had was my heart," Ripmaster said about finishing. After years of trying, Ripmaster didn't just finish the ITI 1,000—he won it.

BUILDING ON TRADITION

The Iditarod Trail Invitational is an annual ultramarathon race across Alaska. Each year, competitors can apply to race in a 350-mile or a 1,000-mile version of the race.

The ITI 1,000 has a northern route and a southern route, which alternate each year.

For the ITI 350, competitors can bike, run, or ski across the trail. Only biking and running are allowed for the ITI 1,000. Both courses start in Anchorage. The ITI 350 ends in McGrath, while the ITI 1,000 goes all the way to Nome.

The race takes place on the Iditarod Trail, which had been used for over 100 years before the race was first run. Sled dogs and mushers used to use the trail to transport goods across the state. Once the snowmobile was invented, mushers and sled dogs were no longer a necessity. To honor the history of the dogs, the Iditarod Trail Sled Dog Race started as a yearly tradition in 1973. Each year, dozens of mushers and their sled dogs race the full 1,000 miles on the Iditarod Trail.

The Iditarod Trail Sled Dog Race became an instant success. As it grew more popular over the years, people began to think of other races to run on the trail. Joe Redington Sr. is known as the father of the Iditarod, as he helped coordinate the first sled dog race in 1973. He even competed in it for years. Then, in 1983, he came up with the idea to have a ski race on the trail. By 1987 there were skiing, biking, and snowshoeing races all held on the trail.

Brave adventurers competed in these unofficial races for years. Bill Merchant was one of those adventurers. After getting support from other regular racers on the trail, he officially formed the ITI in 2002. Since then, the 350- and 1,000-mile races have been held each year.

Having "invitational" in the official name of the race is intentional. Participants must apply to run either of the two races. To be eligible to race in the ITI 350, competitors must have finished two long-distance winter races. There is a list of 12 races that serve as qualifiers for the ITI 350, and they are held in Canada, Finland, Norway, and

northern areas of the United States. To be considered for the ITI 1,000, competitors must first finish the ITI 350. That at least gets them prepared for the harsh conditions of the Iditarod Trail.

TRAINING CAMP

It takes elite levels of endurance and mental strength to finish an ultramarathon. And to finish the ITI, competitors also have to prepare for the brutal conditions that the Alaskan trail provides. While all of the competitors train on their own to get into shape for the race, the ITI offers an official training camp led by experienced instructors in order to prepare competitors for all three forms of the race. Since the ITI presents many dangers to the athletes who compete in it, the camp is not focused on training to win the race. It focuses much more on making sure competitors can survive the course.

It costs $1,200 to enter the training camp. Once the athletes arrive at the camp, they go over

Competitors train on all types of terrain and in different weather conditions to be ready for the challenges of the Iditarod Trail.

how to prepare for the ITI. This includes advice on what gear to bring to the race and what clothing to wear. The trail can get extremely wet and cold. So instructors show the athletes how to protect their faces, hands, and feet from experiencing frostbite. And since athletes must spend some nights sleeping outside during the ITI, they sleep outdoors every single night at the camp.

Nutrition is another key part of the camp. By providing athletes with evening meals, the camp offers a glimpse of what kind of food they'll need during the race. It also provides a time each night when campers and instructors can bond and talk about their experiences with outdoor adventures. On top of tips about the proper food to eat during the race, instructors also teach the athletes how to avoid dehydration while traveling hundreds of miles.

Attending the camp is not a requirement for competing in the ITI. But it is encouraged. The camp is held in February every year. Anyone who

BRING YOUR OWN GEAR

The only help the athletes get at the ITI training camp is the meal that is served each evening. Campers are expected to bring food for themselves for breakfast and lunch each day. The camp provides a list of recommended gear, but the athletes must bring all their own bikes, skis, sleds, and athletic gear to the camp.

Racers pull supplies such as food, a small stove, a sleeping bag, and extra layers of dry clothes.

Competitors pack lots of extra clothing. Wearing the correct clothing can help prevent frostbite.

completes the camp automatically qualifies to compete in the ITI 350 the following year.

SOLO TRAINING

Whether an athlete attends the training camp or not, every person who competes in the ITI does a lot of specific training before the race. And that doesn't mean just biking, running, or skiing long distances. Athletes should train in cold, snowy conditions to get used to what's to come in Alaska.

A native of Saint Cloud, Minnesota, Ben Doom competed in the ITI 350 on his bike in 2015. To prepare for the race, he went on bike rides that ranged from four to eight hours in length. He said that even though he lived in central Minnesota, he had to travel to find areas with more snow to get used to riding with more resistance.

One of the most important parts of getting ready for the ITI is shipping supplies before the race even begins. Competitors in both the ITI 350 and ITI 1,000 must carry all their own survival gear. And while some food is provided at checkpoints, athletes provide most of their own food. In the ITI 1,000, racers are not provided either support or food for the final 500 miles (805 km) of the race.

To avoid carrying a lot of food during the race, athletes ship the food to specific checkpoints. Competitors are

The frozen conditions in the ITI are similar to those experienced during the trail's famous sled dog race. Musher Sonny Lindner tries to stay warm on a particularly cold morning on the Iditarod Trail in 2009.

encouraged to tightly duct-tape boxes that contain food. This is to make sure mice, squirrels, and other animals don't smell the food and eat it all before the athletes get there themselves.

The texture of the snow impacts how quickly competitors can run or ride through it.

OUT IN THE COLD

Any ultramarathon is difficult because of the distance of the race. The biggest challenge in the ITI, however, is the conditions on the trail. The wind can gust up to 120 miles per hour (193 km/h). That can lead to colder temperatures and much slower travel.

The temperature on the trail can range from 35 degrees Fahrenheit (2°C) down to −65 degrees Fahrenheit (−54°C). Warmer weather can lead to the trail becoming slushy and hard to race through. And extreme cold can cause athletes to suffer from frostbite or hypothermia. During the race in 2017, a competitor took off his winter hat to find a piece of his ear attached to the hat due to frostbite.

One of the most challenging parts
of the ITI is dealing with the cold.

Another big challenge the competitors face is navigating the trail itself. Whether an athlete is competing in the 350- or 1,000-mile course, one requirement is that they must stop at every checkpoint on the trail. However, in between checkpoints they can take any path they choose. The trail is not marked.

So competitors rely on Global Positioning System (GPS) devices to make sure they're heading toward the finish line. Sometimes athletes get lost and end up traveling additional miles to get back on track.

NATURAL BEAUTY

Competing in the ITI is a daunting task. But the experience isn't always miserable for the competitors during the race. The trail is in a remote location and features beautiful views of mountains. At night the competitors may see the northern lights. Many competitors are drawn to the ITI for the natural beauty the trail offers.

BEWARE OF ANIMALS

One of the more threatening features of the trail is the wildlife that lives near it. Moose are the most common— and most dangerous—animals that athletes may encounter during the race. If a moose feels threatened by people, it may charge at them, kick them, or stomp on them. Adult moose in Alaska stand 6 feet (183 cm) tall and can range

Some racers use trekking poles to navigate the trail.

from 800 to 1,600 pounds (363 to 726 kg). When these large animals attack, they can cause serious injuries.

Due to heavy snowfall during the 2020 ITI, race organizers cleared a path with snowmobiles. However, moose migrated to the path, in order to avoid areas covered in heavier snow. Once on the cleared trail, the moose refused to leave. Several racers were attacked. Some only had their bikes damaged. Anchorage native Greg Mills wasn't as lucky, though. While skiing on the course, he encountered a moose that nearly knocked him off the trail. He later encountered a second moose that attacked him. The moose kicked Mills into a snowbank and then stomped on him repeatedly. As Mills scrambled backward, he fell into a tree well. He hid there until the moose left after a few hours, and he was fortunate to avoid serious injury.

Finding time to rest can be tough during the race. Competitors don't want to spend too much time not traveling. And the cold wind can make it difficult to get consistent sleep on the trail. Rebecca Rusch competed in the ITI 350 in 2020. After making a wrong turn in the first hour of the race, she needed to make up time. With little time to rest, Rusch started to suffer from sleep deprivation.

While walking on the trail at night, she couldn't see much. The entire landscape blended together. The lack of

Racers carry most of their supplies with them in order to stay warm and nourished on the trail.

sleep caused her to hallucinate. Objects started to appear in the sides of her vision. When she turned her head to look at them, they weren't there. The feeling of extreme fatigue also made her want to sit near the trail to rest. But she knew if she did that, she could freeze to death.

CHAPTER 4

BEATING THE ELEMENTS

Every athlete pays a fee to participate in the ITI. But there is no prize money for winning the race. The first man and woman to finish each discipline of the races wins free entry into the next year's race. There is no reward for anyone else who finishes behind the winners.

Money doesn't serve as a motivator for competing in the ITI. However, some athletes have been able to gain from their experience on the trail. Tyson Flaharty was the men's ITI 350 bike champion in 2019, 2022, and 2023. Racing successes earlier in his career earned him a sponsorship deal with the company 9:Zero:7. Jill Homer has competed in the ITI 350 on bike and on foot. She has written about her experience on the trail in multiple books.

The bikers and runners of the ITI are motivated to finish for the thrill of the challenge, not for a prize.

Just finishing the ITI is a massive accomplishment. In 2023 there were 97 competitors combined between the ITI 350 and ITI 1,000. Thirteen completed the ITI 1,000, 38 completed the ITI 350, and 46 did not finish the race they entered. Fewer racers entered the 2020 event, when the conditions were brutally bad. Only three competitors finished the ITI 1,000 that year.

The challenge just to get to the finish line intrigues a lot of the competitors. And there are many reasons why someone might want to compete in the ITI. Colorado native Eszter Horanyi has said she first attempted the ITI because it was like a puzzle she wanted to solve. Rebecca Rusch finished sixth in the women's ITI 350 in 2021. She said that she learns the most about herself when she experiences pain. The ITI became a teacher for her.

Still, the competitors suffer while they're competing in the ITI. Horanyi admitted that when she competed in

WINNING IS FINISHING

Since the race itself is so grueling, most competitors are not focused on trying to win the event. For a lot of the competitors, the goal is simply to make it to the finish line. John Logar, who won the ITI 1,000 in 2014, once said this about the race: "I was the first person to get to Nome. But we [ultra-athletes] don't really care. Winning is finishing."

The brutal cold challenges racers mentally as well as physically.

27

Racers can become so separated from each other during the ITI that seeing another competitor is an exciting event.

2013, at one point she questioned why she had decided to try the ITI. But once she got to a checkpoint that night, she was laughing while reflecting on her day on the trail, glad to start again the next day. Getting to the finish line is the ultimate test of endurance and mental strength. Another competitor, Amber Bethe, said her initial feeling once she crossed the finish line was one of relief, not celebration.

HOME COOKING

While there is no cash reward for finishing the race, competitors do get to relax in McGrath when they finish the ITI 350. The finish line is the house of Peter and

Tracy Schneiderheinze. Every year since the race started, they have welcomed competitors into their home and given them a place to rest once they've completed the race. The Schneiderheinzes make pancakes for the athletes. And they provide sleeping bags next to fireplaces where the athletes can warm up. This also gives competitors a chance to bond with each other after completing such a draining race.

Some competitors who finish the ITI 350 stay at the house for 24 hours. The athletes competing in the ITI 1,000 rest for a while before continuing their journey. Their finish line is in Nome, which is the same finish line that's used for the Iditarod Sled Dog Race.

Once athletes return home from the ITI, they need time to recover. It can take time for athletes to get back to a normal sleep schedule after completing the race. Bethe finished the ITI 350 in 2020. She said she slept for the majority of the first three days after she returned home. Then it became difficult for her to sleep because aches in her legs would wake her up in the middle of the night. It took her more than two weeks after finishing the race to begin to feel normal again.

The overall experience is daunting for athletes. But once they cross the finish line, they earn their place among the most extreme ultramarathoners in the world. And many of them can't wait to do it again the following year.

GLOSSARY

daunting
Seeming difficult to deal with.

dehydration
A condition in which the body does not have enough water.

endurance
The quality of being able to do something for a long time.

fatigue
Extreme tiredness.

frostbite
Injury to body tissue caused by extreme cold.

hallucinate
To experience something that is not present.

hypothermia
A condition of having low body temperature.

landscape
All the visible features of an outdoor area.

mushers
People who drive dogsleds over snow.

resistance
Forces working against someone or something.

sleep deprivation
Symptoms caused by a lack of sleep.

snowshoeing
Walking on snow in special shoes that prevent a person from sinking into the snow.

ultramarathon
A race lasting longer than the standard marathon distance of 26.2 miles (42.2 km).

BOOKS

Blevins, Haley, and Jennifer Pharr Davis. *Hiking and Camping*. New York: Odd Dot, 2021.

Hewson, Anthony K. *Arrowhead 135*. Minneapolis, MN: Abdo Publishing, 2024.

Miller, Susan Hoskins. *Tour Divide*. Minneapolis, MN: Abdo Publishing, 2024.

ONLINE RESOURCES

To learn more about the Iditarod Trail Invitational, visit **abdobooklinks.com** or scan this QR code. These links are routinely monitored and updated to provide the most current information available.

INDEX

ABOUT THE AUTHOR

Luke Hanlon is a sportswriter and editor based in Minneapolis.